LAUREATE

----------Poems of Vivid Vibrancy ------------

----------- B. Deh.-----------

TROIKA STUDIOS & PUBLISHNG
SALEM, OREGON

*

Laureate: Poems of Vivid Vibrancy

Printed in the United States of America
1ˢᵗ Edition

A special thanks to CreateSpace & Kindle Direct Publishing KDP
For the formatting and quality review. Laurel Wreath cover image by rawpixel.com
All other images from istockphoto.com, non-AI. A Book of Bard; Poemadeh candidate.

ISBN-13: 978-1-966716-04-4
ISBN Hardcover: 978-1-966716-05-1

Troika Studios & Publishng; Salem, Oregon
Printing by KDP; Charlotte, South Carolina; Troutdale, Oregon, USA
An Amazon Company. Member Artists in Action, Oregon Poetry Association

*

*

LAUREATE

Table of Contents

*

*

*

INTRODUCTION
Laureate

A Laureate is a person who has been honored for achieving distinction in a particular field or with a particular award. More importantly, they are representatives- An exemplar of that field and in extension, a representative for that field. By giving my Indian name- Shadow Catcher- my grandmother Lilly bestowed this honor to me.

"Poet" was bestowed by my first audience, and I accept this. In at least to be concise in describing my style of writing. Alternative free verse one may deem. Since its inception, these writings were not ideologies to convince. New notions often pop into mind then I feel compelled to share these as fantastical extrapolations.

John Edge (In My 60's, Look Both Ways) was a Beatnik poet from the San Francisco Bay area who moved to Salem, Oregon. John enabled my title "author" by showing me the ropes of the industry and gave me encouragement with insight. This title is also an homage to "Sir", a youth in New Orleans that legally changed his name, but not his behaviors, to garner respect as a unique person.

Words matter. I would be honored to know if anyone reading this would find it representative of their life or experience. Thank you for reading Laureate.

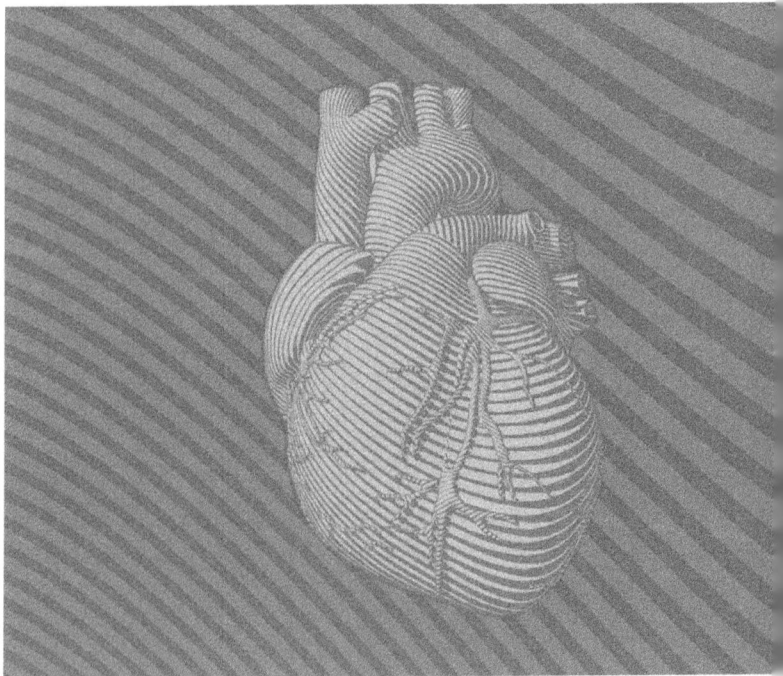

*

If you fret
Do not dread
Make it music

Salem 06.15.24 @1755

*

Cannot put cat
Back in the bag
But the paw prints evaporate
Winds push the bag
And unkeen hands dispose
Unclean minds depose
Yes, they get away
But your own feline
Indelibly marks your mind

Salem 02.05.25 @0158

Teach what is right
Goodness arises
Another will be jealous
One creates beauty
Goodness arises
Ugly retribution follows
When one espouses joy
Another dread severs

Gilchrist, OR 06.09.24 @1251

*

Force the whole world
    Into an uproarious chorus
Fame fleeting
Warships retreating
Die back into obscurity
Everyone with talent
Everyone deserving of praise
All a precious soul

          Salem 05.10.25 @1624

*

Even if not gifted
You can be the gift

Salem 01.24.24

*

Points to a circle
Circular vs linear
Ingredients with
Bullet points
Diameter gauge caliber
At gun point
Magazine round
Draw the line on this globe

Independence, OR 12.27.24 @ 1551

*

When you see me on sun ups
I become your favorite -day of the week

Salem 10.22.24 @1056

*

Recollection, worst is behind us
Read the room
The worst is- remind us

                      Salem 08.26.25 @0727

*

Fantastical mundane
Prayers over dirt and water
Time stamp that tonight
Antidepressant loose joy
The chiaroscuro morning light
On the pedestrian
As you traverse the day

Salem 08.19.25 @0829

*

Blood altered
    Tarnished or purified
First stage to heart change

                        Albany, OR 12.27.24 @1634

*

I swallow
   Nerves erupting upwards
Kite a message

                    Salem 10.25.24 @ 0352

*

In the yellow light
Of cowardice
Sadness appears
As envy

Salem 06.07.25 @1413

*

You are not to
Contest the Shepherd
Nor the
Would-be martyr's meetings

                    Salem 10.25.24 @0401

*

Elected to the summit
Internal votes placed

Salem 10.25.24 @0441

*

The glass half full
The glass half empty
Depending on
Being filled or emptied

Vacaville, CA 1992

Truth of it
Question rather
Take 100 steps
    And recognized for 10,000
Take 10,000 steps
    And recognized for 100
One not the other
Either
Step-and-know, feed
Know-and-step, heed

Salem 01.24.24 @0728

*

Bury my heart at Wounded Knee
Liver in Texas,
    Brain- North Dakota
Lungs- the Nebraska forest
Foot- California,
    Off Travis' Cannon & Bradley
Hand to spouse
Remains- Necropolis

Plunge my eyes off the Pacific Coast
My kidney to my kin
My spirit stays- those places
Petition away my sin
Send off my soul to Heaven
On a chariot of prayer

                    Salem 01.30.24 @1205

*

Analogous underdog
Has yet to set
The precedent

Salem 11.06.23 @0311

*

Hold up!
This is a take over!
Vacancies in Ol' PA,
MA,   MI; NJ   & NM
The poet laureate
Take my lead in the void

                    Snyder, TX 04.20.24 @0047

*

Appease
If those who tell you
It is fine and
Know the problems

Salem 11.12.24 @0806

*

From the stench of defeat
The odor will rise
Foreshadow my comeback

                    Salem 11.13.24 @0319

*

Trade in the routine
Where you need me
To when we hug

                    Salem 11.13.24 @ 0737

*

Rode a cold horse
On the way to Silverado

                    Salem 11.13.24 @ 1501

*

Though in doubt
Appear doughty

Salem 05.11.25 @0126

*

Hear O hero
See R seer
Feel O filio
Affiliate satiation
Taste E morsels

                    Salem 12.17.24 @0427

*

All the wonder wished upon
Cannot realize in time

Salem 12.17.24 @0428

*

Sublime as it was
Was not Heaven
From my state I elevate
Directly solid into vapor
With no intermediary,
No purgative level
Limelight playing me out of myself
Then return because I now know
Not in that elevated state

                          Salem 12.28.24 @0206

Telescope to the sky
Wondering why
I have not found my gold

                    Christmas Valley, OR 03.26.22

Reversable jacket
Invert the whole
Wear us out
Inside-out hoodlum
Hide the eyes
Face away

Salem 10.06.21

*

Finger to a hand
Point, fold, protect, hold
Finger to a had
Insatiable to no eNd

Salem 12.26.24 @1137

*

Wrapped in it
Tend to, attend to another sensation
Another sensation
Trend to
Stay in the parlay
Why must we leave
Better feeling
Like letting go of your lover
So to heal wounds
Unlike

Salem 05.29.22 @0805

*

Eyes always searching
Use always hungry

                    St. Benedict, OR 06.30.24 @1644

*

Stars and Hearts
Stripes and scars
Seem to team
Together
Despite disparate backgrounds
Color the shapes the same

Salem 05.29.22 @1041

*

Not scared of nothing
Then scared of something
Something can be everything

Salem 11.22.22 @0944

*

Unrequited love
Disenchanted spirit
Eternal soul takes score
Flesh and blood turn sore
Remitting weary pain
Unfinished business remain
    Makes ghosts of us all
Move-out-away-from
Any relative grave

                    Salem 11.22.22 @0829

*

No promises
Mayfly
Other than
Short life, will die

Christmas Valley 04.08.22 @2251

*

Traveled the world
North, West
East and South
Running so fast, just to find self
Luggage pack tight, as you moved away
I could wait-lifted off
As you alighted the train
You are here now but
Where are they
The old, they are gone
The new, they await
That is what you told yourself
Surely was not true
A new day dawning on you
Sorely remiss

Salem 03.30.25 @2244

*

We are a small case
Enduring the course
Lowercase path
Lowercase word
Scepter sword
    For us
Sepulcher Word
    For the Greatest

                    Castlerock, WA 04.18.25 @1531

Fission of charity
Stay charitable
Yet incapable of alms
Now that reparations paid

Salem 09.15.23 @2219

*

The book is not ob-seen
It is ob-read
Obliquely believed

                    Salem 09.15.23 @2219

*

The trees have eyes
Swirled in the grain
In place of detached branches
Watch us in the wood
They are knot eyes

Christmas Valley, OR 03.26.22 @2147

*

Out there in the wake. I woke
Voiceless vulnerable
Recognize late mistake. It spoke

Salem 07.02.2020

*

Leaving love clues
Love cues
Much more than a muse
You are my motive
Orienting centrifuge

Salem 04.18.20 @0219

*

Desert land barren
Laid bare our souls

     Christmas Valley, OR 07.04.21 @1234

*

The prayer of my thought
Soul of my being
Nutrient to my crumb
Eternal echoes of my meaning
Never in vain, not in vanity
Penance to my petition
Poem of my penning

Salem 01.20.22 @0314

*

Death
De-life
De vivre
Of life

Salem 01.20.22 @0339

*

What might be a run-on
In prose
Could be a complete journey
In poetry

Salem 01.20.22 @0401

*

Oh I fear
Almighty- protect me from sorrow
Unavoidable, I know
But might you postpone
    Then by my strength
    Not by callous tone
I am told
To bundle my joys
Tight upon my chest

Salem 01.20.22 @0348

*

First the desert exotic
    Outside of you
Then you go, compelled
    Gets on you
Then you rest
    Gets in your bed
In your head
    Between your dreams
Then in you breath
    Gets inside you
Then it is in you

        Christmas Valley, OR 07.29.23 @2215

*

Our projections forecasted
Images of what we may become
Hopes, dreams & other things
But right now is our life

                    Salem 03.10.22 @2357

*

For the briefest of moments
I forgot your death
A nebulous plan
   To see you again
Bent space
Time traveled
Here we are
Temporal immortal
Now in memorial

                    Salem 11.16.18

*

Caught up in raptured splendor
Gain afoot stilled surrender
What number more for that wing to lift
A heart of gratitude is becoming
A hand gathering threads for tailor
Salve, holy, is your
Vocation vintner
That liquid also the
Salve of your pains

Salem 12.09.18

Negotiating with your heart
Screaming out your love language
Giving out your good will
Trusting with blood
Guard dropped vulnerable
It is a gamble
L'artery

Salem 01.11.19

*

Livid, spewing hot piss
Like a torn bladder
Over the detriment

                              Salem 06.07.25 @1410

*

Your heart wasn't pierced
It was compressed
Pressed- held still
By former paramour
I take the title
I hold that word
Again to pulsate
Day by day
Metaphor love
Uncaptured hearts cannot be pierced
If I am to pierce
It's to stint
If I am to press
It's to squeeze and release
Repeated pumping

Salem 02.05.25 @ 0319

*

No need to be brighter
If painting them dark
Makes us appear lighter
Contrast stark

Camas, WA 04.17.22

*

I need to do
What I've been meaning to do
Been putting off
Time to cut the loss
I was oppressed
      So I suppressed
      Became depressed
About everything
I was severing
Go down into the bunker
      Hunker down
Mortification, close eyes
Detest
Debrief
Deep breath
Deep rest

                         Salem 12.14.22 @1804

*

Pleasant hill, pleasant 'til
Met with challenge
Felt mountainous
Die on that hill
Say it was contiguous

Pleasant Hill, OR 04.08.22 @1437

*

Truth shoots right through
May feel like injury
Insincere projectiles
Unserious projections
Defensively formed
Hurled at your body
Can strike the heart
There it lies within your body
Therein changing indelibly

Salem 01.20.24 @0733

*

Largest looming interest
In the smallest detail
The mountain
Takes your fingers
Eats your toes
Everest my pride

Salem 04.13.25 @2351

*

Are we to marry
Or are we just pretending
Things we do together for keeps

Salem 04.13.25 @1946

*

Disagree in premise
Still saying prayers
Distilled animosity
For that soul, cares
Not for their misdeeds

Salem 02.03.25 @2058

*

Feeding off roadkill
At the place of demise
Our haphazard lives
    At hazard

                    Silverlake, OR 06.17.22 @0012

*

Shallowed breaths
Trauma hinders intake
Waited on baited breath
Shut that loaded trap

Salem 02.05.25 @0328

*

I wrote a letter
W
For win, as in win the moment
L
For love, therein I love you
Love letters
        Supersede previous predicament
W/L no matter the result

                              Salem 02.12.25 @0802

*

There is your way
My way, soirees
Highways & byways
Take a dip in that cold spring

Christmas Valley, OR 09.26.2020

*

The confluence
Of you and I
Creates the Y
No longer a question
It is the why
One heading positive north
One due west sun set

Salem 04.13.25 @0202

Smokers be blessed
Gehenna false impression
Sentinels of neighborhood watch

Salem 05.22.16

*

Somehow got on the LA track
    But I do not mind
Want to start slow
See how things go
Hold a conversation or five

             Salem 07.27.16

```
Love is pink
Love is red
Most vibrant colors in my head
Love is white
Love be blue
Love is green
Love in you
```

Portland, OR 11.24.10

*

Greatness
Measured in limitation
Awesome
Too much of a good thing
Awful

                    Salem 02.12.25 @1941

Two tip-touched triangles
Trilogies for time
Analogies align

Salem 10.18.16

*

Love you but got to tell
I've got an electric arcade in the rain
Run on sentences spanning the decade
Got razor burn without taking note
Land locked vessel in a seasonal moat
Please please forgive me
I have nothing to show
For all I've done
For what I know
And all I've failed, felled and razed
For a spell, under the spell
And nothing quell
My druthers

Albany, OR 03.30.25 @1705

*

What abides in you
Determines
Where you build your abode

                    Salem 04.27.24 @1736

*

Long lamented minds dement
Confusion-riddled conscious
Concussive force rattled
Benevolence abandoned
Where have the acts of love gone?

Salem 04.21.2020 @0740

*

Only soul
Save your own
Exceptions accepted
Those who help elevate
    Have your heart in mind

            Junction City, OR 03.30.25 @1613

*

Autonomic system
Heart drums
Blood pumps
I breathe
I swallow
I beat my heart
Consciously

Salem 10.25.24 @0353

*

Prudence repeating
Square circles

                    Salem 07.24.25 @1859

*

Memory belongs to imagination

Portland, OR 11.17.10

*

To-morrow. Fro-morrow,
Two morrow, four morrow
For morrow. From morrow
Tumor, former
Temerity, for marrow

Salem 01.01.22

*

First attracted by the difference
Second we spent time together
Then we became one in the same

                    Salem 05.03.2020

*

We understand through metaphor
45 Parallels
To equate a meaning

Portland, OR 11.22.10

*

Free fall calculator
Best practice
Operate outside the field
Otherwise in the field

                    Salem 01.06.25 @1917

*

Stars
A glittery glamouring
A glimmer of something
Inciting clamoring
Beyond our grasp

Salem 12.09.10 @0530

*

A temporary fix
Turns long term
For seldom used contraptions

                    Salem 03.19.25 @0300

*

Running down the highway
It's running out
It's running out
Name the river after me,
The bridge or the road
Name the mountain or its peak
If not to replace my guilt
In-fill the tomb
It's running out

Christmas Valley, OR 11.22.2020

*

Opposing conclusions
Do not equivocate
One cares & concludes
And
One careless & concludes
Differently

Salem 01.23.25 @0945

*

Idealism thereto reined in
Pragmatism reigns
Even they, able to make out
In the busied figments

Salem 06.07.25 @0204

*

Surprised
Like a knifed sniper

Salem 01.16.21

*

Disputation
Be engaged in the world
Without being
Engaged to the world

Portland, OR 11.23.11

Realize sight limited
Raise awareness
Extrapolate
    Braille

        Salem 02.24.25 @0826

*

Ill deeds preserved in true memory
Stop proclaiming
"It is good"
It is not
Façade
Attempts to layer falsity
Over top

Salem 02.05.25 @0255

*

Professors teaching little brains
Everything around about
    Every subjective topic

                    Salem 01.29.25 @0833

*

Monumental task
To ask
A quiet 3 minutes

                    Portland, OR 11.23.11

*

Passed through my hands
So fast
Some may say
At comedic speed
Confounding my lumbering mind
Preoccupied intelligence divide
Searching to ingest something eternal

Salem 03.23.25 @1803

*

Obesity will always be
A massive problem

Salem 01.15.25 @1337

*

How much fuel burned
To run yellow lights
Downplayed danger
Wrong hue
Even worse
How much folly fuel expended?
To get to
Next inevitable red

Salem 02.12.25 @0828

*

Breathing with purpose
Mouth agape
Eyes a-gate
Words a rapping
Arms akimbo
Defiant to my fate

Portland, OR 12.05.11

*

Ideas clear
Prescient for human movement

Salem 11.12.24 @0233

*

E-vile in e-ville- new community
Repellant, repugnant to goodness
Online technological
One need not know all flavors
      Of feces
The vileness on electronics
Same old disease with new
commutability
Defibrillate the started heart

Salem 02.24.24 @1706

*

She's an echo of goodness
Echo of good?
Echo of good
Most we can hope
To endeavor -echo good
Creators within creation

Salem 04.30.24 @1808

*

Scratched and clawed
Fevered frenzy
Over what?
Platitudes of the decrepit
The plentitude of tortured
     Poets' biographies

                    Snyder, TX 04.20.24 @0107

*

Cold hard cash
Can be tender
Fold for flash
Bought out softened
Sold marred flesh

Salem 02.05.25

*

```
Lost faith
Took life, passed
Take faith
Lose life past
```

Salem 02.24.24 @1705

*

A spider
B spider
C spider
D spider

Salem 07.25.25 @0849

*

For why I write these words
Gather to coagulate
Stop the bleeding
Importance dawning
Shifts actions

Christmas Valley, OR 03.29.25 @2350

*

Alkali lake
Acid lake
Draw the water between them
Break the blockade
Better than brackish
Neutralize to potable

Salem 02.20.25 @1150

*

Blame to my brainless hands
Indiscreet faulty tasks
I don't know I might have
Hit my head
I fell to one side
I believe I'm right

Salem 02.05.25 @0732

*

Roaring at 45
No groaning, no grinding engine
Aging anecdote
Solution youthful

Salem 04.04.25 @1810

*

Got busted at the bottom
Of a neglected pocket
Typically the keenest place
Despite my faulty focus
My pocket will provide
In my most urgent hour

Portland, OR 05.14.25 @0103

*

Do not
Deem divining
What is gleaning

Salem 02.24.25 @1606

*

It's crazy how in my head you are

Salem 08.01.25 @0950

*

Milk and urine
Same person
Different place

                    Salem 08.03.25 @0329

*

Real realm of dragons
Kingdom of dreams
Iliad under the eyelids

Fremont-Winema Forest, OR 04.27.25 @1201

*

We never mean never
Labile current condition

                    Salem 08.01.25 @0848

*

Stadium sounds in my basement
Rumbling ground under feet
Entire earth in purview
Play that pained punk rock
Chrome-tone guitar
Golden voice, silver tongued
It's been a long, long grind
For a long, long time
Projecting for all
Overshot any one heart

Salem 11.20.22 @1952

*

Close your eyes
Down your mouth
Hold hand gestures
Keep in words
Shut your lies up

Corvallis, OR 07.25.24 @1644

*

I kept it to myself
Kept at it
Kept it all

Salem 11.20.22 @2147

*

Do not believe me
Send in the orderlies

Salem 03.26.25 @0228

*

All those hail Mary's
Lofted up into the sky
Somethings got to land

                          Salem 03.26.25 @1102

*

Setting sun flushed all
Monochromatic
Orange ablazened
Indistinguishable from gold

  Fremont-Winema Forest, OR 06.16.22 @2333

*

Night falls
Rueful heart quakes
Then day breaks
Radiantly emits
Silver light hits
Then suspended in dawn
Splendid in twilight

Salem 12.20.19 @0708

*

So sad now
That happy sound
In contrast to where
I currently dwell

     Fort Rock, OR 03.25.22 @1654

Gnashing teeth
Prefer gashing

    Christmas Valley, OR 02.21.25 @2041

*

May all your hopes hold weight
All your dreams take flight

Salem 12.21.19

*

NOTES

wards and Honors

- January- December 2025- Contest Host; Syzygy International Poetry Prize 2025. Approximately 47,416 Participants and Contestant submissions by this publication

- October 2025- Random Genius Award, The Anything Writing Contest;   (As Classical Music; Syzygy, 2020). Presented by: Sehaj Saksham SoHoJZ; Kathua, India.

- October 2025- Gold Star Liked It Award, Fan Poetry Writing Contest; (Flowing Down Our Street; Laureate, 2025). Presented by: Alan Dietrich, United States of America

- October 2025- Honorable Mention Award, The Anything Writing Contest; (The Sky Is Blue; Cantus, 2010). Presented by: Sehaj Saksham SoHoJZ; Kathua, India.

- August 2025- 1,500 Points Earned with special impact on the community. Writer's Café Badge of Honor

- November 2024- Top Writer; Badge of Honor Recipient, receiving over 50 positive reviews with overall rating 95% or higher

- June 2023- Lauded Award, Backburner Poems Contest; Writer's Café (Prudent Purveyor, Cantus, 2010). Presented by Red Brick Kreshner; Brisbane, West Moreton, Australia

- February 2023- Top Reviewer; Badge of Honor Recipient, provided over 100 critical reviews

- November 2022- Singular Award, Imitating Imitation Writing Contest; Writer's Café (Of Something Great, Cantus, 2010). Cogito Group; Presented by Swagato Saha; Kolkata India

- November 2022- Badge of Honor. Contest winner from Writerscafe.org

- November 2022- Particular Award, Imitating Imitation Writing Contest; Writer's Café (Ability Falls to Will, Cantus, 2010). Cogito Group; Presented by Swagato Saha; Kolkata India

- July 2022- Honorific title 'Laird' from Eddleston, Scotland (ET3122468 located at 55° 44' 29.0446190664" N, -3° 15' 21.26161382148" W)

- December 2021- 'I Welcome New Writers' Badge of Honor; Writerscafe.org

- March 2015 — Hero Award, Salem Health; Salem Hospital ICU Medical Social Worker

- January 2015 — Hero Award, Salem Health; Salem Hospital ICU Medical Social Worker

- December 2014 — Team Award, Salem Health; Salem Hospital ICU Medical Social Worker

*

*

Thank you

*

www.ingramcontent.com/pod-product-compliance
Lightning Source LLC
Chambersburg PA
CBHW020508040426
42331CB00042BA/81